To

Sherry

From

Dee — 2005

Happy Birthday!

BRIGHTENERS™

Celebrating Women

365 Day Brighteners™ Celebrating Women
Copyright © 2004 DaySpring® Cards, Inc.
Published by Garborg's®, a brand of DaySpring® Cards, Inc.
Siloam Springs, Arkansas
www.dayspring.com

Except for Scripture verses, references to men and masculine pronouns have been replaced with "people," "women," and gender-neutral or feminine pronouns.

Scripture quotations are from the following sources: The HOLY BIBLE, NEW INTERNATIONAL VERSION® (NIV®) © 1973, 1978, 1984 by International Bible Society. Used by permission of Zondervan Publishing House. THE MESSAGE © Eugene H. Peterson 1993, 1994, 1995. Used by permission of NavPress Publishing Group. All rights reserved. The Living Bible (TLB) © 1971 by permission of Tyndale House Publishers, Inc., Wheaton, IL. The New Revised Standard Version of the Bible (NRSV) © 1989 Division of Christian Education, National Council of Churches. Used by permission of Zondervan Publishing House.

ISBN 1-58061-968-1
Printed in China

365 DAY BRIGHTENERS™

BRIGHTENERS™

Celebrating Women

GARBORG'S®

because every day is a gift

*A*llow your dreams a place
in your prayers and plans. God-given
dreams can help you move into
the future He is preparing for you.

Barbara Johnson

January 1

*I*n today's world…it is still women's business to make life better, to make tomorrow better than today.

HELEN THAMES RALEY

January 2

*E*ach one of us is God's
special work of art. Through us,
He teaches and inspires, delights
and encourages, informs and uplifts
all those who view our lives.

JONI EARECKSON TADA

January 3

*L*iving in the past is a dull and
lonely business; looking back strains
the neck muscles, causes you to bump
into people not going your way.

EDNA FERBER

January 4

$\mathcal{G}$od has given each of you some
special abilities; be sure to use them to
help each other, passing on to others
God's many kinds of blessings.

1 PETER 4:10 TLB

January 5

*M*any women...have buoyed me
up in times of weariness and stress.
Each friend was important.... Their
words have seasoned my life.
Influence, just like salt shaken out, is
hard to see, but its flavor
is hard to miss.

PAM FARREL

January 6

$\mathcal{I}$ believe that we are always attracted to what we need most, an instinct leading us toward the persons who are to open new vistas in our lives and fill them with new knowledge.

HELENE ISWOLSKI

$\mathcal{F}$ace your deficiencies and
acknowledge them; but do not let
them master you. Let them teach you
patience, sweetness, insight.
When we do the best we can,
we never know what miracle is
wrought in our life, or in the
life of another.

HELEN KELLER

$\mathcal{J}$anuary 8

The moral climate of our world depends greatly on the stature of its women.

BEVERLY LaHAYE

January 9

This is my prayer: that your love
will flourish and that you will not only
love much but well. Learn to love
appropriately. You need to use
your head and test your feelings
so that your love is sincere
and intelligent, not sentimental gush.

PHILIPPIANS 1:9-10 THE MESSAGE

January 10

$\mathcal{J}$f we had no winter, the spring would not be so pleasant: if we did not sometimes taste of adversity, prosperity would not be so welcome.

ANNE BRADSTREET

January 11

$\mathcal{B}$oth within the family
and without, our sisters hold up our
mirrors, our images of who we are
and of who we can dare to become.

ELIZABETH FISHEL

January 12

$\mathcal{H}$aving someone who
understands is a great blessing
for ourselves. Being someone
who understands is a great
blessing to others.

JANETTE OKE

January 13

The real joy of life is in its play.
Play is anything we do for the joy
and love of doing it, apart from any
profit, compulsion, or sense of duty.
It is the real living of life with
the feeling of freedom and
self-expression. Play is the business
of childhood, and its continuation in
later years is the prolongation
of youth.

WALTER RAUSCHENBUSCH

January 14

$\mathcal{W}$hat you say goes, God,
and stays, as permanent
as the heavens. Your truth never
goes out of fashion; it's as up-to-date
as the earth when the sun
comes up. Your Word and truth
are dependable as ever.

PSALM 119:89-91 THE MESSAGE

January 15

$\mathcal{W}$e have ample evidence that
the Lord is able to guide.
The promises cover every
imaginable situation. All we
need to do is to take
the hand He stretches out.

Elisabeth Elliot

January 16

$\mathcal{W}$hen you least expect it,
a common thread—golden,
at that—begins to weave together
the fabric of friendship.

MARY KAY SHANLEY

January 17

$\mathcal{S}$urely we ought to prize
those friends on whose principles
and opinions we may constantly
rely—of whom we may say
in all emergencies, "I know
what they would think."

HANNAH FARNHAM LEE

January 18

Opinion is a flitting thing,
But Truth outlasts the Sun—
If then we cannot own them both—
Possess the oldest one.

EMILY DICKINSON

January 19

The right word at the right time
is like a custom-made piece of jewelry,
and a wise friend's timely reprimand
is like a gold ring slipped
on your finger.

PROVERBS 25:11-12 THE MESSAGE

January 20

$\mathcal{T}$here are times when
encouragement means such a lot.
And a word is enough to convey it.

January 21

$\mathcal{G}$od puts each fresh morning,
each new chance of life,
into our hands as a gift to see
what we will do with it.

January 22

$\mathcal{T}$rue contentment is a real,
even an active, virtue—not only
affirmative but creative.
It is the power of getting out
of any situation all there is in it.

G. K. CHESTERTON

$\mathcal{J}$anuary 23

$\mathcal{G}$ood habits are not made
on birthdays, nor Christian character
at the new year. The workshop
of character is everyday life.
The uneventful and commonplace
hour is where the battle is lost or won.

MALTBIE D. BABCOCK

$\mathcal{J}$anuary 24

*I*f you don't know what you're
doing, pray to the Father. He loves
to help. You'll get his help,
and won't be condescended to when
you ask for it. Ask boldly, believing,
without a second thought.

JAMES 1:5-6 THE MESSAGE

January 25

$\mathcal{I}$ have attempted to convey...
a message, which God has given,
and to convey that message with
whatever abilities were given to me.
Whatever I've been able to accomplish
has been God's doing. I've tried
to follow His teachings in all
my writing and thoughts.

GRACE LIVINGSTON HILL

$\mathcal{J}$anuary 26

One thing I realized about having
a girlfriend is that I can't tell you who
I am without telling you who my
girlfriend is. Our relationships with
other women are part of the ground
of our being. So I can't say who I am
without talking about my female friend
and who she is in my life. We discover
ourselves through our girlfriends;
it's a mutual process of self-discovery.

SUE MONK KIDD

January 27

$\mathcal{S}$ervice is the rent we each pay for living. It is not something to do in your spare time; it is the very purpose of life.

MARIAN WRIGHT EDELMAN

$\mathcal{J}$anuary 28

$\mathcal{V}$irtue shows quite as well
in rags and patches as she does
in purple and fine linen.

CHARLES DICKENS

January 29

*C*harm is deceptive, and beauty
is fleeting; but a woman who fears
the Lord is to be praised.

PROVERBS 31:30 NIV

January 30

$\mathcal{L}$iving is the constant adjustment of thought to life and life to thought in such a way that we are always growing, always experiencing new things in the old and old things in the new.

THOMAS MERTON

$\mathcal{J}$anuary 31

*W*hen we live life centered around
what others like, feel, and say,
we lose touch with our own identity.
I am an eternal being, created by God.
I am an individual with purpose.
It's not what I get from life, but who
I am, that makes the difference.

NEVA COYLE

February 1

$\mathcal{N}$othing we can do will make
the Father love us less; nothing we
do can make Him love us more.
He loves us unconditionally with
an everlasting love. All He asks of us
is that we respond to Him with
the free will that He has given to us.

NANCIE CARMICHAEL

February 2

$\mathcal{W}$hen we put people before
possessions in our hearts,
we are sowing seeds
of enduring satisfaction.

BEVERLY LAHAYE

$\mathcal{F}ebruary$ 3

*A*nd God is able to make all grace
abound to you, so that in all things
at all times, having all that you need,
you will abound in every good work.

2 CORINTHIANS 9:8 NIV

February 4

$\mathcal{N}$ot everyone possesses
boundless energy or a conspicuous
talent. We are not equally blessed
with great intellect or physical
beauty or emotional strength.
But we have all been given
the same ability to be faithful.

GIGI GRAHAM TCHIVIDJIAN

February 5

$\mathcal{F}$riendship with oneself
is all-important, because without
it one cannot be friends with
anyone else in the world.

ELEANOR ROOSEVELT

$\mathcal{F}$ebruary 6

$\mathcal{N}$o one lights a lamp, then hides it in a drawer. It's put on a lamp stand so those entering the room have light to see where they're going. Your eye is a lamp, lighting up your whole body. If you live wide-eyed in wonder and belief, your body fills up with light.... Keep your eyes open, your lamp burning, so you don't get musty and murky. Keep your life as well-lighted as your best-lighted room.

LUKE 11:33-36 THE MESSAGE

$\mathcal{F}$ebruary 7

Choices can change our lives
profoundly. The choice to mend
a broken relationship, to say "yes"
to a difficult assignment, to lay aside
some important work to play with
a child, to visit some forgotten
person—these small choices
may affect our lives eternally.

GLORIA GAITHER

February 8

*C*ake delight in the Lord, and he
will give you the desires of your heart.

PSALM 37:4 NRSV

February 9

$\mathcal{W}$isdom is knowing what
to do next, skill is knowing how
to do it, and virtue is doing it.

DAVID STARR JORDAN

$\mathcal{F}$ebruary 10

To love what you do and feel
that it matters—how could
anything be more fun?

KATHARINE GRAHAM

February 11

I am not bound to win,
but I am bound to be true:
I am not bound to succeed,
but I am bound to live
up to what light I have.

ABRAHAM LINCOLN

February 12

A good friend will sharpen
your character, draw your soul
into the light, and challenge your
heart to love in a greater way.

February 13

$\mathcal{T}$he steadfast love of the Lord never ceases, his mercies never come to an end; they are new every morning; great is your faithfulness.

LAMENTATIONS 3:22-23 NRSV

February 14

*N*o love, no friendship can
cross the path of our destiny without
leaving some mark on it forever.

FRANÇOIS MAURIAC

February 15

*J*ust don't give up trying
to do what you really want to do.
Where there is love and inspiration,
I don't think you can go wrong.

ELLA FITZGERALD

February 16

*L*ife begins each morning....
Each morning is the open door
to a new world—new vistas,
new aims, new tryings.

LEIGH HODGES

February 17

*L*ive as though you believe that
the power behind the universe
is a power of love, a personal power
of love, a love so great that all
of us really do matter to Him.

MADELEINE L'ENGLE

$\mathscr{I}$f I rise on the wings of the dawn,
if I settle on the far side of the sea,
even there your hand will guide me,
your right hand will hold me fast.

PSALM 139:9-10 NIV

$\mathscr{F}$ebruary 19

*B*less every humble soul who,
in these days of stress and strain,
preaches sermons without words.

PETER MARSHALL

February 20

$\mathcal{I}$t is a good thing to be rich,
and a good thing to be strong,
but it is a better thing
to be loved of many friends.

EURIPIDES

$\mathcal{F}$ebruary 21

$\mathcal{I}$ have learned from experience
that the greater part of our happiness
or misery depends on our dispositions
and not on our circumstances.

MARTHA WASHINGTON

$\mathcal{F}ebruary$ 22

*O*ur brightest blazes of gladness
are commonly kindled
by unexpected sparks.

SAMUEL JOHNSON

February 23

$\mathcal{T}$he Lord is good to all,
and his compassion is over
all that he has made.

PSALM 145:9 NRSV

$\mathcal{F}$ebruary 24

*I*f you treat an individual
as if she were what she ought to be
and could be, she will become what
she ought to be and could be.

February 25

I always prefer to believe
the best of everybody—it saves
so much trouble.

RUDYARD KIPLING

February 26

$\mathcal{F}$riends that hold each other accountable usually have a deep, abiding, and open relationship.... Being aware that a friend cares enough to make us accountable creates a stronger bond.

$\mathcal{F}ebruary$ 27

A kind heart is a fountain
of gladness, making everything
in its vicinity freshen into smiles.

WASHINGTON IRVING

February 28

$\mathcal{W}$hen she speaks, her words
are wise, and kindness is the rule
for everything she says.

PROVERBS 31:26 TLB

February 29

$\mathcal{W}$e must know that we have
been created for greater things,
not just to be a number in the world,
not just to go for diplomas and
degrees, this work and that work.
We have been created in order
to love and to be loved.

MOTHER TERESA

$\mathcal{A}$s God's workmanship,
we deserve to be treated,
and to treat ourselves,
with affection and affirmation,
regardless of our appearance
or performance.

MARY ANN MAYO

March 2

$\mathcal{H}$ave patience with all things,
but chiefly have patience with yourself.
Do not lose courage in considering
your own imperfections but instantly
set about remedying them—every
day begin the task anew.

FRANCIS DE SALES

$\mathcal{M}$arch 3

$\mathcal{W}$omen of adventure have
conquered their fates and know how
to live exciting and fulfilling lives right
where they are. They have learned
to reinvent themselves and find
creative ways to enjoy the world and
their place in it. They know how
to take mini-vacations, stop and smell
the roses, and live fully in the moment.

BARBARA JENKINS

$\mathcal{M}arch$ 4

*L*ive out your God-created
identity. Live generously
and graciously toward others,
the way God lives toward you.

MATTHEW 5:48 THE MESSAGE

March 5

$\mathscr{I}$ am convinced beyond
a shadow of any doubt that
the most valuable pursuit we can
embark upon is to know God.

KAY ARTHUR

March 6

$\mathcal{I}$f you believe in a God who
controls the big things, you have
to believe in a God who controls
the little things. It is we, of course,
to whom things look "little" or "big."

ELISABETH ELLIOT

March 7

$\mathcal{T}$oo often the I-can-handle-it-myself
society we live in seems to promote
loneliness rather than friendship.
Friends are an important part of sharing
the burden and worry of each day.

SHERI CURRY

So where do you go when you can't fix your life? The only place to go is back to the One who made you.

Sheila Walsh

March 9

$\mathscr{S}$teep yourself in God-reality,
God-initiative, God-provisions.
You'll find all your everyday human
concerns will be met. Don't be afraid
of missing out. You're my dearest
friends! The Father wants to give
you the very kingdom itself.

LUKE 12:31-32 THE MESSAGE

March 10

Every day under the sun is a gift.
Receive it with eagerness.
Treat it kindly. Share it with joy.
Each night return it to the Giver
who will make it bright and shiny
again before the next sunrise.

March 11

There is an exquisite melody
in every heart. If we listen closely,
we can hear each other's song. A
friend knows the song in your heart
and responds with beautiful harmony.

March 12

$\mathcal{B}$e dependable...to yourself
as well as others. Know that others
can depend on you to do what you
promise to or need to. And depend
on yourself to do something
that pleases you each and every day.

KATHY PEEL

March 13

$\mathcal{I}$t isn't the big pleasures
that count the most; it's making
a great deal out of the little ones.

JEAN WEBSTER

March 14

*H*ow precious it is, Lord,
to realize that you are thinking
about me constantly! I can't even
count how many times a day
your thoughts turn towards me.

PSALM 139:17-18 TLB

March 15

$\mathcal{T}$he glory of friendship is found
in the inspiration that comes
when I discover that someone
else believes in me and is willing
to trust me with their friendship.

March 16

$\mathscr{E}$verything in life is most
fundamentally a gift.
And you receive it best,
and you live it best, by holding
it with very open hands.

LEO O'DONOVAN

March 17

*G*irlfriends are those women
who know us better than anyone
(sometimes better than we know
ourselves). They are not only essential
for coping with our day-to-day
frustrations or sharing private jokes,
they help us limp through a crisis
and, in the long run, help us grow
as women and human beings.

CARMEN RENEE BERRY AND TAMARA TRAEDER

March 18

$\mathcal{S}$ome people are so special that
once they enter your life, it becomes
richer and fuller and more wonderful
than you ever thought it could be.

March 19

$\mathcal{Y}$ou're blessed when you care.
At the moment of being "care-full,"
you find yourselves cared for.
You're blessed when you get
your inside world—your mind
and heart—put right. Then you can
see God in the outside world.

MATTHEW 5:7-8 THE MESSAGE

$\mathcal{M}$arch 20

$\mathcal{T}$he fountain of beauty is the heart,
and every generous thought illustrates
the walls of your chamber.

FRANCIS QUARLES

March 21

$\mathcal{S}$ome of the most rewarding
and beautiful moments of a friendship
happen in the unforeseen open spaces
between planned activities.
It is important that you allow
these spaces to exist.

CHRISTINE LEEFELDT

$\mathcal{M}$arch 22

$\mathcal{T}$he people who get on
in this world are the people who
get up and look for the
circumstances they want,
and, if they can't find them,
make them.

GEORGE BERNARD SHAW

$\mathcal{M}$arch 23

$\mathcal{A}$ friend and I flew south with our children. During the week we spent together I took off my shoes, let down my hair, took apart my psyche, cleaned the pieces, and put them together again in much improved condition. I feel like a car that's just had a tune-up. Only another woman could have acted as the mechanic.

ANNA QUINDLEN

March 24

$\mathcal{A}$s far as God is concerned
there is a sweet, wholesome fragrance
in our lives. It is the fragrance
of Christ within us.

2 CORINTHIANS 2:15 TLB

March 25

Sometimes it is a slender thread,
Sometimes a strong, stout rope;
She clings to one end,
I the other;
She calls it friendship;
I call it hope.

LOIS WYSE

March 26

$\mathcal{S}$omething deep in all of us yearns
for God's beauty, and we can
find it no matter where we are.

SUE MONK KIDD

March 27

$\mathcal{W}$hat a circus we women
perform every day of our lives.
It puts a trapeze artist to shame.

ANNE MORROW LINDBERGH

March 28

*B*eing a good friend, and having
a good friend, can enrich your days
and bring you lifelong satisfaction.

SUE BROWN

March 29

$\mathcal{W}$hat happens when we live God's way? He brings gifts into our lives, much the same way that fruit appears in an orchard—things like affection for others, exuberance about life, serenity. We develop a willingness to stick with things, a sense of compassion in the heart, and a conviction that a basic holiness permeates things and people.

GALATIANS 5:22 THE MESSAGE

$\mathcal{M}$arch 30

$\mathcal{M}$y fondest hope is that I may
be worthy of a place in your friendship, and being admitted to that sacred
circle, that I may never prove
unfaithful to your trust in me.

EDWIN OSGOOD GROVER

March 31

$\mathcal{W}$ise sayings often fall
on barren ground; but a kind
word is never thrown away.

Sir Arthur Helps

$\mathcal{A}pril$ 1

$\mathcal{I}$f your lips can speak a word
of encouragement to a weary soul,
you have a talent.

EVA J. CUMMINGS

April 2

$\mathcal{A}$ppreciate the goodness of God.
Count your blessings. Learn not
to take benefits, endowments
and pleasures for granted; learn
to thank God for them all.

J. I. PACKER

$\mathcal{A}pril$ 3

$\mathcal{T}$he Lord is good, a refuge
in times of trouble. He cares
for those who trust in him.

NAHUM 1:7 NIV

$\mathcal{A}pril\ 4$

$\mathcal{I}$f you can help anybody even
a little, be glad; up the steps
of usefulness and kindness,
God will lead you on to happiness
and friendship.

MALTBIE D. BABCOCK

April 5

The beauty of a woman is not in
the clothes she wears,
The figure that she carries,
or the way she combs her hair.
The beauty of a woman must be seen
from in her eyes,
Because that is the doorway to her heart,
the place where love resides.

AUDREY HEPBURN

April 6

$\mathcal{W}$e the willing, led by
the unknowing, are doing
the impossible for the ungrateful.
We have done so much with so little
for so long, we are now qualified
to do anything with nothing.

April 7

*I*t is pleasing to the dear God
whenever you rejoice or laugh
from the bottom of your heart.

MARTIN LUTHER

April 8

*J*esus cannot forget us; we have
been graven on the palms of His
hands.

LOIS PICILLO

I demand that you love each other
as much as I love you. And here
is how to measure it—the greatest love
is shown when a person lays down
his life for his friends.

JOHN 15:12-13 TLB

April 9

Our confidence in the future is based firmly on the fact of what God has done for us in Christ. No matter what our situation may be, we need never despair because Christ is alive.

BILLY GRAHAM

April 10

$\mathcal{T}$he yes of Easter is the most
welcome word we hear all year.
It is our alleluia.

CHERYL FORBES

April 11

There is something very powerful
about...someone believing in you,
someone giving you another chance.

SHEILA WALSH

April 12

$\mathcal{K}$ind words are jewels that live
in the heart and soul and remain
as blessed memories years after
they have been spoken.

MARVEA JOHNSON

April 13

$\mathcal{L}$et [God] have all your worries
and cares, for he is always
thinking about you and watching
everything that concerns you.

1 PETER 5:7 TLB

April 14

$\mathcal{I}$t is often just as sacred
to laugh as it is to pray.

April 15

$\mathcal{N}$o person can tell whether
she is rich or poor by turning
to her ledger. It is the soul that makes
a person rich. She is rich or poor
according to what she is, and not
according to what she has.

HENRY WARD BEECHER

April 16

$\mathcal{A}$ span of life is nothing.
But the man or woman who lives that
span, they are something. They can
fill that tiny span with meaning,
so its quality is immeasurable, though
its quantity may be insignificant.

CHAIM POTOK

April 17

$\mathcal{W}$e cannot rebuild the world
by ourselves, but we can have a small
part in it by beginning where we are.
It may only be taking care
of a neighbor's child or inviting
someone to dinner, but it is important.

DONNA L. GLAZIER

April 18

*N*ow glory be to God,
who by his mighty power at work
within us is able to do far more than
we would ever dare to ask or even
dream of—infinitely beyond
our highest prayers, desires,
thoughts, or hopes.

EPHESIANS 3:20 TLB

April 19

$\mathcal{A}$s women, we want to know
we are important and that we have
a significant place in our world.
We need to know that we matter
to someone, that our lives are making
a difference in the lives of other
people, that we are able to touch
their souls. This desire to have
value is God-given.

BEVERLY LaHAYE

April 20

$\mathcal{S}$ome people, no matter how old
they get, never lose their beauty.
They merely move it from their
faces to their hearts.

BARBARA JOHNSON

April 21

$\mathcal{N}$otice words of compassion.
Seek out deeds of kindness.
These are like the doves from heaven,
pointing out to you who are the ones
blessed with inner grace and beauty.

CHRISTOPHER DE VINCK

April 22

$\mathcal{W}$hat we lack is not so much
leisure to do as time to reflect
and time to feel. What we seldom
"take" is time to experience
the things that have happened,
the things that are happening,
the things that are still ahead of us.

MARGARET MEAD AND RHODA METRAUX

April 23

The Lord will guide you always;
he will satisfy your needs
in a sun-scorched land.... You will
be like a well-watered garden,
like a spring whose waters never fail.

ISAIAH 58:11 NIV

April 24

*F*aith is the first factor
in a life devoted to service.
Without faith, nothing is possible.
With it, nothing is impossible.

Mary McLeod Bethune

April 25

*W*hat constitutes success?
She has achieved success who has
lived well; laughed often and loved
much; who has gained the respect
of intelligent people and the love
of little children; who has filled her
niche and accomplished her task; who
has left the world better than she
found it; who has always looked for
the best in others and given
the best she had.

BESSIE ANDERSON STANLEY

April 26

The ordinary acts we practice every day at home are of more importance to the soul than their simplicity might suggest.

SIR THOMAS MORE

April 27

$\mathcal{M}$ay God send His love like
sunshine in His warm and gentle way,
To fill each corner of your heart
each moment of today.

$\mathcal{A}$pril 28

*W*hat matters is not your outer appearance—the styling of your hair, the jewelry you wear, the cut of your clothes--but your inner disposition. Cultivate inner beauty, the gentle, gracious kind that God delights in.

1 PETER 3:3-4 THE MESSAGE

April 29

$\mathcal{S}$ome blessings—like rainbows
after rain or a friend's listening ear—
are extraordinary gifts waiting
to be discovered in an ordinary day.

April 30

*G*od's promises are intended
not to supersede, but to excite
and encourage our prayers.

MATTHEW HENRY

$\mathcal{W}$e teach by our words, by our *talk*. But we also teach by our walk— by the way we live our life. Our walk encompasses all that we do and say and all that we don't do and don't say.

ELIZABETH GEORGE

God's wisdom is always available
to help us choose from alternatives
we face, and help us to follow
His eternal plan for us.

GLORIA GAITHER

$\mathcal{N}$o test or temptation that comes
your way is beyond the course of what
others have had to face. All you need
to remember is that God will never
let you down; he'll never let you
be pushed past your limit; he'll always
be there to help you come through it.

1 CORINTHIANS 10:13 THE MESSAGE

May 4

$\mathcal{T}$he things we are going through
are either making us sweeter, better,
nobler men and women; or they
are making us more captious
and fault-finding, more insistent upon
our own way. The things that happen
either make us fiends, or they make
us saints; it depends entirely upon
the relationship we are in to God.

OSWALD CHAMBERS

From quiet homes
and first beginning
Out to the undiscovered ends.
There's nothing worth
the wear of winning,
But laughter and the love of friends.

HILAIRE BELLOC

May 6

$\mathcal{I}$ cannot count the number
of times I have been strengthened
by another woman's heartfelt hug,
appreciative note, surprise gift,
or caring questions.... My friends
are an oasis to me, encouraging
me to go on. They are essential
to my well-being.

DEE BRESTIN

To act lovingly is to begin to feel loving, and certainly to act joyfully brings joy to others, which in turn makes one feel joyful. I believe we are called to the duty of delight.

DOROTHY DAY

May 8

On Mother's Day, I think moms
should be able to wake up and say to
themselves: I'm not just a housewife,
I'm a domestic goddess!

BARBARA JOHNSON

Her children stand and bless her;
so does her husband. He praises her.

PROVERBS 31:28 TLB

May 9

$\mathcal{N}$o relationship affects
us more than our relationship
with our mother.... If that primary
relationship with mother is positive
we learn how to be good women
and good friends at the same time.
Or are these the same thing?

CARMEN RENEE BERRY AND TAMARA TRAEDER

May 10

$\mathscr{M}$ore and more I realize
that everybody, regardless of age,
needs to be hugged and comforted
in a brotherly or sisterly way now
and then. Preferably now.

JANE HOWARD

May 11

$\mathcal{T}$he healthiest relationships
are those that "breathe"—that is,
they move out from one another
for a few days and then come back
together for a time of closeness.

JAMES DOBSON

May 12

$\mathcal{B}$lessed are they who have
the gift of making friends,
for it is one of God's best gifts.

THOMAS HUGHES

$\mathcal{M}ay$ 13

$\mathcal{S}$ay only what is good and helpful
to those you are talking to,
and what will give them a blessing.

EPHESIANS 4:29 TLB

May 14

There's something much more important than taking time and effort to make our outer being as lovely as possible. We can tighten our stomach muscles and suck it up, pay a plastic surgeon to tuck it up, or spend a lot of money trying to dress it up, but unless we are growing beautiful on the inside, our efforts to be glamorous on the outside are useless.

KATHY PEEL

May 15

The way you keep your house,
the way you organize your time,
the care you take in your personal
appearance, the things you
spend your money on all speak
loudly about what you believe.

ELISABETH ELLIOT

May 16

$\mathcal{G}$iving is the secret of a healthy
life...not necessarily money,
but whatever a person has
of encouragement and sympathy
and understanding.

JOHN D. ROCKEFELLER JR.

$\mathcal{M}ay$ 17

Slow down awhile! Push aside
the press of the immediate. Take time
today, if only for a moment, to lovingly
encourage each one in your family.

GARY SMALLEY AND JOHN TRENT

May 18

*W*hen we love each other
God lives in us, and his love
within us grows ever stronger.

1 JOHN 4:12 TLB

May 19

$\mathcal{I}$t is always wise to stop wishing
for things long enough to enjoy
the fragrance of those now flowering.

PATRICE GIFFORD

May 20

$\mathcal{W}$e should look for reasons
to celebrate—a raise, a promotion,
an A on a paper—even
a good hair day.

PAM FARREL

May 21

The most universally awesome
experience that mankind knows
is to stand alone on a clear night
and look at the stars. It was God who
first set the stars in space; He is their
Maker and Master.... Such are His
power and His majesty.

J. I. PACKER

May 22

*W*henever you are asked
if you can do a job, tell 'em,
"Certainly I can!" Then get busy
and find out how to do it.

THEODORE ROOSEVELT

May 23

$\mathcal{Y}$ou are my lamp, O Lord;
the Lord turns my darkness
into light. With your help I can
advance against a troop;
with my God I can scale a wall.

2 SAMUEL 22:29-30 NIV

May 24

*C*haracter cannot be developed
in ease and quiet. Only through
experience of trial and suffering
can the soul be strengthened,
vision cleared, ambition inspired,
and success achieved.

HELEN KELLER

May 25

$\mathcal{M}$ay your footsteps set you
upon a lifetime journey of love.
May you wake each day with His
blessings and sleep each night
in His keeping. And may you
always walk in His tender care.

May 26

That is God's call to us—simply
to be people who are content
to live close to Him and to renew
the kind of life in which the closeness
is felt and experienced.

THOMAS MERTON

May 27

$\mathcal{H}$ow blessed I am that I can walk beside you, lean upon you, and live within the warmth of your love.

ROY LESSIN

$\mathcal{M}ay\ 28$

$\mathcal{E}$ven if you're on the right track,
you'll get run over if you just sit there.

WILL ROGERS

Steady plodding brings prosperity.

PROVERBS 21:5 TLB

May 29

$\mathcal{A}$ life without contemplation quickly loses depth. It becomes like a field that is all top-soil—one strong wind and it is all blown away. It is of no long-term use to anyone. Thought, reflection, engaging of the mind—these are all what it takes if we are to have something to say...if our ideas are to be clear, concise, and well developed.

RUTH SENTER

May 30

$\mathcal{F}$riendships begun in this world
can be taken up again in heaven,
never to be broken off.

FRANCIS DE SALES

$\mathcal{M}ay$ 31

$\mathcal{W}$e may...depend upon God's promises, for...He will be as good as His word. He is so kind that He cannot deceive us, so true that He cannot break His promise.

MATTHEW HENRY

June 1

$\mathcal{N}$o tool, in and of itself,
has great importance. But placed
in the proper hands it can
create a masterpiece.

JONI EARECKSON TADA

$\mathcal{J}$une 2

$\mathcal{Y}$et the Lord still waits for you
to come to him so he can show you his
love; he will conquer you to bless you,
just as he said. For the Lord is faithful
to his promises. Blessed are all those
who wait for him to help them.

ISAIAH 30:18 TLB

June 3

$\mathscr{E}$very act of kindness
Moves to a larger one
'Til friendships bloom to show
What little deeds have done.

JUNE MASTERS BACHER

$\mathscr{J}$une 4

$\mathcal{W}$e must not, in trying to think about how we can make a big difference, ignore the small daily differences we can make which, over time, add up to big differences that we often cannot foresee.

MARIAN WRIGHT EDELMAN

$\mathcal{J}$une 5

$\mathcal{W}$hen you were born, you cried
and the world rejoiced. Live your life
in such a manner that when you die,
the world cries and you rejoice.

INDIAN PROVERB

$\mathcal{J}$une 6

$\mathscr{B}$eing a good friend, and having a good friend, can enrich your days and bring you lifelong satisfaction. But friendships don't just happen. They have to be created and nurtured. Like any other skill, building friendship has to be practiced.

Sue Browder

June 7

The Lord is wonderfully good
to those who wait for him,
to those who seek for him.
It is good both to hope and wait
quietly for the salvation of the Lord.

LAMENTATIONS 3:25-26 TLB

June 8

$\mathcal{H}$e cannot bless us unless
He has us. When we try to keep within
us an area that is our own, we try
to keep an area of death. Therefore,
in love, He claims all.

C. S. LEWIS

$\mathcal{J}$une 9

*H*ealed by Your love, corruption
and decay are turned, and whole,
we greet the light of day.

MADELEINE L'ENGLE

But for you who fear my name,
the Sun of Righteousness will rise
with healing in his wings.

MALACHI 4:2 TLB

June 10

There may be no trumpet sound
or loud applause when we make
a right decision, just a calm sense
of resolution and peace.

GLORIA GAITHER

June 11

The daisy was glad to stand out in the grass…it felt very grateful; and when the sun went down it folded its leaves and went to sleep, and dreamed all night about the sun.

HANS CHRISTIAN ANDERSEN

June 12

$\mathcal{B}$e...full of sympathy toward
each other, loving one another with
tender hearts and humble minds.

1 PETER 3:8 TLB

June 13

$\mathcal{F}$or generations women
have affected the values and character
of their families with sewing
and needlework. It seems to me that
part of our culture has literally
been carried on a needle—gliding
in and out of our lives, pulling
a thread of beauty as well as duty.

SANDY LYNAM CLOUGH

June 14

*T*rust your friends with both
the delightful and the difficult
parts of your life.

LUCI SHAW

June 15

$\mathscr{I}$t doesn't take monumental feats
to make the world a better place.
It can be as simple as letting someone
go ahead of you in a grocery line.

BARBARA JOHNSON

$\mathscr{J}$une 16

$\mathcal{F}$riendship is like love at its best: not blind but sympathetically all-see-ing; a support which does not wait for understanding; an act of faith which does not need, but always has, reason.

LOUIS UNTERMEYER

June 17

*E*very single act of love bears
the imprint of God.

*My beloved friends, let us continue to love
each other since love comes from God.
Everyone who loves is born of God and
experiences a relationship with God.*

1 JOHN 4:7 THE MESSAGE

June 18

$\mathcal{Y}$ou have a unique message
to deliver, a unique song to sing,
a unique act of love to bestow.
This message, this song, and this
act of love have been entrusted
exclusively to the one and only you.

JOHN POWELL

$\mathcal{S}$uccess is often possible
only with intense action
accompanied by persistent will.
Persistence is taking one more step.

PAM FARREL

$\mathcal{J}$une 20

$\mathcal{E}$ating lunch with a friend. Trying to do a decent day's work. Hearing the rain patter against the window. There is no event so commonplace but that God is present within it, always hiddenly, always leaving you room to recognize Him or not to recognize Him.

FREDERICH BUECHNER

June 21

*O*riginality is not doing something
no one else has ever done, but doing
what has been done countless times
with new life, new breath.

MARIE CHAPIAN

June 22

*I*n everything you do,
put God first, and he will direct you
and crown your efforts with success.

PROVERBS 3:6 TLB

$\mathcal{T}$rust God where you cannot trace Him. Do not try to penetrate the cloud He brings over you; rather look to the bow that is on it. The mystery is God's; the promise is yours.

JOHN MACDUFF

June 24

There is no surprise more
magical than the surprise of being
loved. It is the finger of God
on a person's shoulder.

MARGARET KENNEDY

$\mathcal{I}$t is my calling to treat every
human being with grace
and dignity, to treat every person,
whether encountered in a palace
or a gas station, as a life
made in the image of God.

<small>SHEILA WALSH</small>

$\mathcal{J}$une 26

*F*riends...lift our spirits,
keep us honest, stick with
us when times are tough,
and make mundane tasks enjoyable.
No wonder we want to make friends.

EM GRIFFIN

June 27

$\mathcal{D}$on't lose a minute in building on what you've been given, complementing your basic faith with good character, spiritual understanding, alert discipline, passionate patience, reverent wonder, warm friendliness, and generous love, each dimension fitting into and developing the others.

2 PETER 1:5 THE MESSAGE

$\mathcal{J}$une 28

*L*ife varies its stories.
Time changes everything,
yet what is truly valuable—what
is worth keeping—is beyond time.

RUTH SENTER

$\mathcal{I}$t is a good and safe rule
to sojourn in every place as if you
meant to spend your life there,
never omitting an opportunity
of doing a kindness, or speaking
a true word, or making a friend.

JOHN RUSKIN

$\mathcal{J}$une 30

$\mathcal{W}$omen don't want a divided
life.... They recognize that career
is not enough; they want
to be interconnected with people.
They want to keep growing
throughout their lives, adjusting
as needed to different circumstances.
They want to live a balanced life.

MARY ELLEN ASHCROFT

July 1

$\mathcal{F}$riends are an indispensable
part of a meaningful life.
They are the ones who share
our burdens and multiply
our blessings.

BEVERLY LaHaye

$\mathcal{J}$uly 2

$\mathcal{F}$inally...whatever is true,
whatever is honorable, whatever
is right, whatever is pure, whatever
is lovely, whatever is of good
repute, if there is any excellence
and if anything worthy of praise,
let your mind dwell on these things.

PHILIPPIANS 4:8 NASB

$\mathcal{J}uly$ 3

The private and personal blessings
we enjoy, the blessings of immunity,
safeguard, liberty, and integrity,
deserve the thanksgiving
of a whole life.

JEREMY TAYLOR

July 4

$\mathcal{G}$od speaks to the crowd, but His
call comes to individuals, and through
their personal obedience He acts.
He does not promise them nothing
but success, or even final victory in
this life.... God does not promise that
He will protect them from trials,
from material cares, from sickness,
from physical or moral suffering.
He promises only that He will
be with them in all these trials,
and that He will sustain them
if they remain faithful to Him.

PAUL TOURNIER

$\mathcal{J}$uly 5

$\mathcal{T}$he miracles of nature do not seem miracles because they are so common. If no one had ever seen a flower, even a dandelion would be the most startling event in the world.

July 6

$\mathscr{I}$ count your friendship one
of the chiefest pleasures of my life,
a comfort in time of doubt and trouble, a joy in time of prosperity and
success, and an inspiration at all times.

EDWIN OSGOOD GROVER

$\mathcal{July}$ 7

The Lord is my strength
and my shield; my heart trusts
in him, and I am helped.

PSALM 28:7 NIV

July 8

$\mathcal{Y}$ou are God's created
beauty and the focus of His
affection and delight.

JANET L. WEAVER

$\mathcal{J}$uly 9

*T*here is no duty we so much
underrate as the duty of being happy.
By being happy we sow anonymous
benefits upon the world.

ROBERT LOUIS STEVENSON

July 10

Open your hearts to the love God
instills.... God loves you tenderly.
What He gives you is not to be kept
under lock and key, but to be shared.

MOTHER TERESA

July 11

$\mathscr{J}$oyfulness keeps the heart
and face young. A good laugh
makes us better friends with
ourselves and everybody around us.

ORISON SWETT MARDEN

July 12

$\mathcal{A}$sk and it will be given to you;
seek and you will find; knock
and the door will be opened to you.
For everyone who seeks finds;
and to him who knocks
the door will be opened.

MATTHEW 7:7-8 NIV

$\mathcal{J}$uly 13

$\mathcal{W}$e have been in God's thought
from all eternity, and in His creative
love, His attention never leaves us.

MICHAEL QUOIST

July 14

_F_or lovely eyes,
Seek out the good in people.
For a slim figure,
Share your food with the hungry.
For beautiful hair,
Let a child run his or her fingers
through it once a day.
For poise,
Walk with the knowledge you'll
never walk alone.

AUDREY HEPBURN

July 15

Through the eyes of our friends,
we learn to see ourselves...through
the love of our friends, we learn
to love ourselves...through the caring
of our friends, we learn what it means
to be ourselves completely.

July 16

Something deep in all of us yearns
for God's beauty, and we can find
it now matter where we are.

SUE MONK KIDD

July 17

$\mathcal{N}$ow you're dressed in a new
wardrobe. Every item of your new way
of life is custom-made by the Creator,
with his label on it. All the old fashions
are now obsolete…. From now
on everyone is defined by Christ,
everyone is included in Christ.

COLOSSIANS 3:10-11 THE MESSAGE

July 18

*I*t is an extraordinary and beautiful
thing that God, in creation...works
with the beauty of matter; the reality
of things; the discoveries of the senses,
all five of them; so that we, in turn,
may hear the grass growing;
see a face springing to life in love
and laughter.... The offerings
of creation...our glimpses of truth.

MADELEINE L'ENGLE

July 19

A friend is one who joyfully
sings with you when you are on
the mountain top, and silently walks
beside you through the valley.

WILLIAM A. WARD

July 20

*I*nto all our lives, in many simple, familiar, homely ways, God infuses this element of joy from the surprises of life, which unexpectedly brighten our days, and fill our eyes with light.

LONGFELLOW

July 21

$\mathcal{G}$od has a wonderful plan for each
person.... He knew even before
He created this world what beauty
He would bring forth from our lives.

LOUIS B. WYLY

$\mathcal{J}$uly 22

$\mathcal{Y}$ou will keep in perfect peace
him whose mind is steadfast,
because he trusts in you.

ISAIAH 26:3 NIV

$\mathcal{J}$uly 23

*Friends...they cherish
each other's hopes. They are
kind to each other's dreams.*

HENRY DAVID THOREAU

July 24

*H*appiness is intrinsic,
it's an internal thing. When you build
it into yourself, no external
circumstances can take it away.

LEO BUSCAGLIA

July 25

$\mathcal{M}$ay you always find three
welcomes in life,
In a garden during summer,
At a fireside during winter,
And whatever the day or season
In the kind eyes of a friend.

$\mathcal{J}$uly 26

$\mathcal{W}$hen we recall the past,
we usually find that
it is the simplest
things—not the great
occasions—that in
retrospect give off the
greatest glow of happiness.

BOB HOPE

July 27

*Y*our right hand,
O Lord, supports me;
your gentleness
has made me great.

PSALM 18:35 TLB

July 28

$\mathcal{N}$o one can arrive from being
talented alone. God gives talent,
work transforms talent into genius.

ANNA PAVLOVA

July 29

*G*od created us with
an overwhelming desire to soar....
He designed us to be tremendously
productive and "to mount up with
wings like eagles," realistically
dreaming of what He can do
with our potential.

CAROL KENT

July 30

$\mathcal{I}$nfluence often isn't noticed
until it blossoms later in the garden
of someone else's life. Our words and
actions may land close to home,
or they may be carried far and wide.

PAM FARREL

July 31

$\mathcal{L}$ isten to your life. See it for
the fathomless mystery that it is.
In the boredom and pain of it no less
than in the excitement and gladness:
touch, taste, smell your way
to the holy and hidden heart
of it because in the last analysis
all moments are key moments
and life itself is grace.

FREDERICH BUECHNER

August 1

$\mathcal{N}$o eye has seen, nor ear heard,
nor the human heart conceived,
what God has prepared
for those who love him.

1 CORINTHIANS 2:9 NRSV

$\mathcal{A}$ugust 2

*H*ospitality is making
your guests feel at home even
though you wish they were.

BARBARA JOHNSON

August 3

$\mathcal{W}$holehearted, ready laughter
heals, encourages, relaxes anyone
within hearing distance. The laughter
that springs from love makes wide
the space around—gives room
for the loved one to enter in.

EUGENIA PRICE

August 4

Our world is hungry for genuinely
changed people. Leo Tolstoy observed,
"Everybody thinks of changing
humanity and nobody thinks
of changing himself." Let us be among
those who believe that the inner
transformation of our lives is a goal
worthy of our best effort.

RICHARD J. FOSTER

August 5

$\mathcal{T}$he tests of this life are to make,
not break us. Trouble may demolish
a man's business but build up
his character. The blow
at the outward man may be
the great blessing to the inner man.

Maltbie D. Babcock

August 6

*W*hen we obey him, every path
he guides us on is fragrant with
his loving-kindness and his truth.

PSALM 25:10 TLB

August 7

$\mathcal{I}$'d like to be the sort of friend that
you have been to me.
I'd like to be the help that you've been
always glad to be;
I'd like to mean as much to you
each minute of the day
As you have meant, old friend of mine,
to me along the way.

EDGAR A. GUEST

August 8

$\mathscr{P}$art of our job is simply
to be...always attentive to what we
are doing and what is going on inside
us, at the same time we listen and pay
attention to the people and events
around us. Part of our job is to expect
that, if we are attentive and willing,
God will "give us prayer," will give
us the things we need, "our daily
bread," to heal and grow in love.

ROBERTA BONDI

August 9

$\mathcal{W}$e are never more fulfilled
than when our longing for God
is met by His presence in our lives.

BILLY GRAHAM

August 10

The secret of joy in work
is contained in one word—excellence.
To know how to do something
well is to enjoy it.

PEARL S. BUCK

August 11

$\mathcal{W}$e walk without fear, full of hope
and courage and strength to do His
will, waiting for the endless good
which He is always giving as fast as He
can get us able to take it in.

GEORGE MACDONALD

August 12

$\mathcal{I}$ have been qualified for
the King's service, not because
of how great I am or what I have
done, but because of how great
Jesus is and what He has done.

Neva Coyle

August 13

$\mathcal{T}$he overflowing life does not just happen. It is only as our own deep thirst is quenched, only as we are filled ourselves, that we can be channels through which His overflow reaches other lives.

GRACE STRICKER DAWSON

August 14

*D*ear friends, no matter how we
find them, are as essential to our lives
as breathing in and breathing out.

LOIS WYSE

August 15

$\mathcal{L}$earn the blessedness
of the unoffended in the face
of the unexplainable.

AMY CARMICHAEL

$\mathcal{A}ugust\ 16$

*T*hough I am surrounded
by troubles, you will bring me safely
through them.... Your power will save
me. The Lord will work out his plans
for my life—for your loving-kindness,
Lord, continues forever.

PSALM 138:7-8 TLB

August 17

$\mathcal{J}$esus is in the boat with us,
no matter how wild the storm is,
and He is at peace. He commands
us not to be afraid.

ELISABETH ELLIOT

August 18

$\mathcal{G}$od not only knows us, but He
values us highly in spite of all
He knows. "You are worth more
than many sparrows."... You and I are
the creatures He prizes above
the rest of His creation. We are
made in His image and He sacrificed
His Son that each one of us might
be one with Him. Sparrows are sold
at two for a penny; we were bought
with a much higher price.

JOHN FISCHER

August 19

$\mathscr{B}$lessed is she who has learned
to laugh at herself, for she shall
never cease to be entertained.

JOHN BOWELL

August 20

$\mathcal{A}$ true friend is one who
is concerned about what we
are becoming, who sees beyond
the present relationship, and who cares
deeply about us as a whole person.

GLORIA GAITHER

$\mathcal{A}ugust$ 21

$\mathcal{B}$e kind to one another, tenderhearted, forgiving one another, as God in Christ has forgiven you.

EPHESIANS 4:32 NRSV

$\mathcal{A}$ugust 22

$\mathcal{W}$alk and talk and work
and laugh with your friends,
but behind the scenes,
keep up the life of simple prayer
and inward worship.

THOMAS R. KELLY

August 23

Some people come into our lives
and quickly go. Some stay for a while
and leave footprints on our hearts
and we are never the same.

August 24

*H*appiness is being at peace,
being with loved ones, being
comfortable. But most of all,
it's having those loved ones.

JOHNNY CASH

August 25

The wonder of our Lord is that He is so accessible to us in the common things of our lives: the cup of water...breaking of the bread... welcoming children into our arms... fellowship over a meal...giving thanks. A simple attitude of caring, listening, and lovingly telling the truth.

NANCIE CARMICHAEL

August 26

A wise person gets known
for insight; gracious words add
to one's reputation.

PROVERBS 16:21 THE MESSAGE

August 27

*A*s I look back, I am convinced
that the whole ordeal of my paralysis
was inspired by His love. I wasn't
in a rat maze. I wasn't the brunt
of some cruel divine joke. God had
reasons behind my suffering,
and learning some of them has made
all the difference in the world.

JONI EARECKSON TADA

August 28

$\mathscr{R}$ecognizing who we are in Christ
and aligning our life with God's
purpose for us gives a sense
of destiny.... It gives form
and direction to our life.

JEAN FLEMING

August 29

$\mathcal{A}$n inexhaustible good nature
is one of the most precious gifts
of heaven, spreading itself like oil over
the troubled sea of thought,
and keeping the mind smooth
and equable in the roughest weather.

WASHINGTON IRVING

August 30

*B*ecause of their agelong training
in human relations—for that is what
feminine intuition really is—women
have a special contribution to make
to any group enterprise.

MARGARET MEAD

August 31

To enjoy your work and to accept your lot in life—that is indeed a gift from God. The person who does that will not need to look back with sorrow on his past, for God gives him joy.

ECCLESIASTES 5:20 TLB

September 1

$\mathcal{W}$hatever job I perform—whether
changing a diaper, closing a deal,
teaching a class, or writing a book—
when I meet legitimate needs,
I am carrying on God's work.

KATHY PEEL

September 2

$\mathcal{I}$t is God's love for us that He
not only gives us His Word but also
lends us His ear. So it is His work
that we do for our sister
when we learn to listen to Him.

DIETRICH BONHOEFFER

September 3

*A*s a rose fills a room with
its fragrance, so will God's love
fill our lives.

MARGARET BROWNLEY

September 4

"Come ye yourselves apart...
and rest a while" (Mark 6:31)
is a must for every Christian. If you
don't come apart, you will come
apart—you'll go to pieces!

VANCE HAVNER

September 5

$\mathcal{B}$ut from everlasting
to everlasting the Lord's love
is with those who fear him,
and his righteousness
with their children's children.

PSALM 103:17 NIV

$\mathcal{S}$eptember 6

$\mathcal{W}$e can receive love even
when we feel unlovable.
It's a choice we make.

LOU ANN SMITH

September 7

This era will pass so quickly,
and the present stresses will seem
insignificant and remote. What will
matter to you at the end of life
will be the loving relationships
you built with your family and your
readiness to meet the Lord.

JAMES DOBSON

September 8

$\mathcal{H}$eroic women know their
purpose in life is not to satisfy their
own desires, but to minister healing,
love, and hope to the less fortunate.

BEVERLY LAHAYE

$\mathcal{S}eptember\ 9$

*C*ourage...is when you know
you're licked before you begin,
but you begin anyway and you
see it through no matter what.

September 10

"*For* I know the plans I have for you," declares the Lord, "plans to prosper you and not to harm you, plans to give you hope and a future."

JEREMIAH 29:11 NIV

September 11

*H*earts never lose touch;
friendships linger forever in a place
that no words could ever describe.

September 12

$\mathcal{K}$nowing what to say is not
always necessary; just the presence
of a caring friend can make
a world of difference.

SHERI CURRY

September 13

The beauty of the earth, the beauty
of the sky, the order of the stars,
the sun, the moon...their very
loveliness is their confession of God.

AUGUSTINE

September 14

$\mathcal{T}$o have a friend is to have one
of the sweetest gifts that life
can bring; to be a friend
is to have a solemn and tender
education of soul from day to day.

September 15

$\mathcal{T}$wo are better than one,
because they have a good return
for their work: If one falls down,
his friend can help him up.

September 16

$\mathcal{W}$e all stumble, every one
of us. That's why it's a comfort
to go hand in hand.

EMILY KIMBROUGH

September 17

$\mathscr{S}$eeing how God works
in nature can help us understand
how He works in our lives.

JANETTE OKE

September 18

$\mathcal{B}$e to the world a sign
that while we as Christians
do not have all the answers,
we do know and care
about the questions.

BILLY GRAHAM

September 19

$\mathcal{I}$ found the sun for me this morning. I thank you, Lord. I found the warm water in the shower. I praise You. I found the bread in my kitchen this morning, Lord. I thank You. I found the fresh air as I stood out the door. I praise You. For all that I see that You do for me, I thank You. For all that I do not see that You do for me, I praise You.

CHRISTOPHER DE VINCK

September 20

$\mathcal{B}$ear with each other
and forgive whatever grievances
you may have against one another.
Forgive as the Lord forgave you.

Colossians 3:13 niv

September 21

The best friendships have
weathered misunderstandings
and trying times. One of the secrets
of a good relationship
is the ability to accept the storms.

ALAN LOY MCGINNIS

September 22

There are two kinds of people in the world: those who come into a room and say, "Here I am!" and those who come in and say, "Ah, there you are!"

September 23

*G*etting things accomplished
isn't nearly as important
as taking time for love.

JANETTE OKE

September 24

$\mathcal{G}$od wants us to be present where we are. He invites us to see and to hear what is around us and, through it all, to discern the footprints of the Holy.

RICHARD J. FOSTER

September 25

$\mathcal{D}$ear friend, guard Clear Thinking
and Common Sense with your life;
don't for a minute lose sight of them.
They'll keep your soul alive and well,
they'll keep you fit and attractive.

PROVERBS 3:21-22 THE MESSAGE

$\mathcal{S}eptember\ 26$

$\mathcal{L}$ove is like a violin.
The music may stop now and then,
but the strings remain forever.

JUNE MASTERS BACHER

September 27

$\mathcal{G}$ ratitude makes sense of our past,
brings peace for today, and creates
vision for tomorrow.

MELODY BEATTIE

September 28

$\mathcal{I}$f you have a special need
today, focus your full attention
on the goodness and greatness
of your Father rather than on the size
of your need. Your need is so small
compared to His ability to meet it.

September 29

$\mathcal{T}$uck [this] thought into your
heart today. Treasure it.
Your Father God cares about your
daily everythings that concern you.

KAY ARTHUR

September 30

$\mathcal{M}$ay your unfailing love rest
upon us, O Lord, even as we
put our hope in you.

PSALM 33:22 NIV

October 1

All the things in this world
are gifts and signs of God's love
to us. The whole world
is a love letter from God.

PETER KREEFT

October 2

*W*ind, rain, falling leaves
of autumn,
Winter snow, springing flow'rs,
and the sunshine
Forth the light of Your love;
countless blessings from above,
As from season to season in You
we live and move—
Moved to praise You always
For the brightness
You pour on our way.

JACK HAYFORD

October 3

Whenever we realize we have not taken advantage of a magnificent opportunity, we are apt to sink into despair. Let the past sleep, but let it sleep in the sweet embrace of Christ, and let us go on into the invincible future with Him. Never let the sense of past failure defeat your next step.

OSWALD CHAMBERS

October 4

The Lord doesn't always remove
the sources of stress in our lives...but
He's always there and cares for us.
We can feel His arms around
us on the darkest night.

JAMES DOBSON

October 5

$\mathcal{Y}$ou're my place of quiet retreat;
I wait for your Word to renew
me...therefore I lovingly embrace
everything you say.

PSALM 119:114,119 THE MESSAGE

October 6

$\mathcal{G}$od is never in a hurry but spends years with those He expects to greatly use. He never thinks the days of preparation too long or too dull.

L. B. COWMAN

October 7

$\mathcal{T}$aken separately, the experiences
of life can work harm and not good.
Taken together, they make a pattern
of blessing and strength the like
of which the world does not know.

V. RAYMOND EDMAN

October 8

$\mathscr{A}$t the sound of a child's pure laugh or the sight of a father holding his baby for the first time, incredible joy pushes upward, spilling over. Our hearts were made for joy. Our hearts were made to enjoy the One who created them. Too deeply planted to be much affected by the ups and downs of life, this joy is a knowing and a being known by our Creator. He sets our hearts alight with radiant joy.

October 9

*A*ll the world is an utterance
of the Almighty. Its countless beauties,
its exquisite adaptations,
all speak to you of Him.

PHILLIPS BROOKS

October 10

$\mathcal{L}$et everything he has made give praise to him. For he issued his command, and they came into being; he established them forever and forever. His orders will never be revoked.

PSALM 148:5-6 TLB

October 11

$\mathcal{G}$od moves in a mysterious way
His wonders to perform;
He plants His footsteps in the sea,
And rides upon the storm.

WILLIAM COWPER

October 12

*R*eputation is what folks think you are. Personality is what you seem to be. Character is what you really are.

ALFRED ARMAND MONTAPERT

*I*f I take care of my character, my reputation will take care of itself.

DWIGHT L. MOODY

October 13

$\mathcal{E}$ncouragement is awesome.
It has the capacity to lift a man's
or woman's shoulders. To spark
the flicker of a smile on the face
of a discouraged child. To breathe
fresh fire into the fading embers
of a smoldering dream. To actually
change the course of another human
being's day, week, or life.

CHARLES SWINDOLL

October 14

$\mathscr{I}$f I could reach up and hold a star
for every time you've made me smile,
the entire evening sky
would be in the palm of my hand.

October 15

$\mathcal{H}$e will give you, through
his great power, everything
you need for living a truly good life:
he even shares his own glory
and his own goodness with us!

2 PETER 1:3 TLB

October 16

$\mathcal{O}$nce an old woman at my church said the secret is that God loves us exactly the way we are and that He loves us too much to let us stay like this. I'm just trying to trust that.

ANNE LAMOTT

October 17

*O*ur Heavenly Father never takes anything from His children unless He means to give them something better.

GEORGE MUELLER

October 18

$\mathcal{G}$rasp the fact that God is for you—let this certainty make its impact on you in relation to what you are up against at this very moment; and you will find in thus knowing God as your sovereign protector, irrevocably committed to you in the covenant of grace, both freedom from fear and new strength for the fight.

J. I. PACKER

October 19

*T*ruth is the secret of eloquence
and of virtue, the basis of moral
authority; it is the highest
summit of art and of life.

HENRI FRÉDÉRIC AMIEL

October 20

$\mathcal{C}$ling to wisdom—she will protect you. Love her—she will guard you. Getting wisdom is the most important thing you can do! And with your wisdom, develop common sense and good judgment.

PROVERBS 4:6-7 TLB

October 21

The first requirement for growth
in self understanding is an unswerving
commitment to honesty with one's self.
No one can break our chains for us,
we have to do this for ourselves.

ELIZABETH O'CONNOR

October 22

$\mathcal{B}$ut God has promised
strength for the day,
Rest for the labor, light for the way,
Grace for the trials, help from above,
Unfailing sympathy, undying love.

ANNIE JOHNSON FLINT

October 23

$\mathcal{W}$e are not capable of perfection;
we will make mistakes and hit many
false notes before this life is through.
But the Lord doesn't give up on us,
and we don't have to achieve
perfection before He can use us.

GIGI GRAHAM TCHIVIDJIAN

October 24

The trouble with being
an optimist is that people think
you don't know what's going on.

October 25

*M*ay God who gives patience,
steadiness, and encouragement
help you to live in complete
harmony with each other.

ROMANS 15:5 TLB

October 26

*I*t's usually through our hard times, the unexpected and not-according-to-plan times, that we experience God in more intimate ways. We discover an unquenchable longing to know Him more. It's a passion that isn't concerned that life fall within certain predictable lines, but a passion that pursues God and knows He is relentless in His pursuit of each one of us.

October 27

$\mathcal{W}$e do not understand the intricate pattern of the stars in their courses, but we know that He who created them does, and that just as surely as He guides them, He is charting a safe course for us.

BILLY GRAHAM

October 28

$\mathcal{G}$ratitude unlocks the fullness
of life. It turns what we have into
enough, and more.... It can turn a meal
into a feast, a house into a home,
a stranger into a friend. It turns
problems into gifts, failures
into successes, the unexpected
into perfect timing, and mistakes
into important events.

MELODY BEATTIE

October 29

$\mathcal{W}$orry does not empty
tomorrow of its sorrow; it empties
today of its strength.

CORRIE TEN BOOM

October 30

$\mathcal{S}$o, chosen by God for this new life of love, dress in the wardrobe God picked out for you: compassion, kindness, humility, quiet strength, discipline.

COLOSSIANS 3:12 THE MESSAGE

October 31

*I*f we just give God the little
that we have, we can trust Him
to make it go around.

GLORIA GAITHER

November 1

$\mathcal{J}$oy is elusive.... It flows most freely when we stop trying to make it happen. We do not come to joy. Joy comes to us.

RUTH SENTER

$\mathcal{N}$ovember 2

Feeling grateful or appreciative of someone or something in your life actually attracts more of the things that you appreciate and value into your life. And, the more of your life that you like and appreciate, the healthier you'll be. Science is now documenting what women have known intuitively for millennia: that "thinking with your heart" will lead you in the right direction.

CHRISTIANE NORTHRUP

November 3

I thank God for my handicaps,
for, through them, I have found
myself, my work, and my God.

HELEN KELLER

November 4

$\mathcal{D}$on't become so well-adjusted
to your culture that you fit into
it without even thinking. Instead, fix
your attention on God. You'll be
changed from the inside out. Readily
recognize what he wants from you,
and quickly respond to it. Unlike
the culture around you, always
dragging you down to its level
of immaturity, God brings
the best out of you, develops
well-formed maturity in you.

ROMANS 12:2 THE MESSAGE

$\mathcal{N}$ovember 5

*T*roubles are often the tools
by which God fashions
us for better things.

HENRY WARD BEECHER

November 6

All that we have and are is one
of the unique and never-to-be-repeated
ways God has chosen to express
Himself in space and time. Each of us,
made in His image and likeness,
is yet another promise He has made
to the universe that He will continue
to love it and care for it.

BRENNAN MANNING

November 7

$\mathcal{G}$od gave me my gifts.
I will do all I can to show Him
how grateful I am to Him.

GRACE LIVINGSTON HILL

$\mathcal{N}$ovember 8

$\mathcal{T}$hank God for dirty dishes;
They have a tale to tell.
While other folks go hungry,
We're eating pretty well.
With home, and health, and happiness,
We shouldn't want to fuss;
For by this stack of evidence,
God's very good to us.

November 9

$\mathcal{L}$et us outdo each other
in being helpful and kind to each
other and in doing good.

HEBREWS 10:24 TLB

November 10

$\mathcal{I}$f you laugh a lot,
when you get older your wrinkles
will be in the right places.

$\mathcal{N}$ovember 11

*H*umor is not a trick,
not jokes. Humor is a presence
in the world—like grace—
and shines on everybody.

GARRISON KEILLOR

November 12

$\mathcal{I}$f we learn how to give
of ourselves, to forgive others,
and to live with thanksgiving,
we need not seek happiness.
It will seek us.

November 13

$\mathcal{L}$ittle acts of kindness which
we render to each other in everyday
life, are like flowers by the way-side
to the traveler: they serve
to gladden the heart and relieve
the tedium of life's journey.

EUNICE BATHRICK

November 14

The Lord your God...will take
great delight in you, he will quiet
you with his love, he will rejoice
over you with singing.

ZEPHANIAH 3:17 NIV

November 15

$\mathcal{I}$t is easy to love those who are far away. It isn't always easy to love those who are right next to us. It is easier to offer a dish of rice to satisfy the hunger of a poor person, than to fill up the loneliness and suffering of someone lacking love in our own family.

MOTHER TERESA

November 16

$\mathcal{W}$hether we are poets or parents
or teachers or artists or gardeners,
we must start where we are
and use what we have. In the process
of creation and relationship,
what seems mundane and trivial
may show itself to be holy,
precious, part of a pattern.

Luci Shaw

$\mathcal{N}ovember\ 17$

*A*lways be in a state
of expectancy, and see that
you leave room for God
to come in as He likes.

OSWALD CHAMBERS

November 18

$\mathscr{G}$race and gratitude belong together
like heaven and earth. Grace evokes
gratitude like the voice an echo.
Gratitude follows grace as thunder
follows lightning.

KARL BARTH

$\mathscr{N}ovember\ 19$

$\mathcal{E}$very detail of your body and soul—even the hairs of your head!—is in my care; nothing of you will be lost.

LUKE 21:18 THE MESSAGE

$\mathcal{N}$ovember 20

$\mathscr{D}$on't assume that you're always
going to be understood. I wrote
in a column that one should put
a cup of liquid in the cavity
of a turkey when roasting it.
Someone wrote me that "the turkey
tasted great, but the plastic cup
melted." So now I say, "Pour a cup...."

HELOISE

$\mathscr{N}$ovember 21

$\mathcal{G}$od provides resting places
as well as working places. Rest, then,
and be thankful when He brings you,
wearied, to a wayside well.

L. B. COWMAN

November 22

$\mathcal{H}$ands down, Thanksgiving
is my favorite holiday. It highlights
the home and family. It is synonymous
with stuff that can be found only
at home—early morning fussing
around in the kitchen,
kids and grandkids,
long distance phone calls,
holding hands and praying
before that special meal.

CHARLES SWINDOLL

November 23

$\mathcal{I}$f you stop to be kind, you must swerve often from your path.

MARY WEBB

November 24

$\mathcal{L}$ et us sing him psalms of praise.
For the Lord is a great God, the great
King of all gods. He controls
the formation of the depths
of the earth and the mightiest
mountains; all are his.
He made the sea and formed the land;
they too are his. Come kneel before
the Lord our Maker, for he is our God.
We are his sheep and he is our
Shepherd. Oh, that you would hear
him calling you today and
come to him!

PSALM 95: 2-7 TLB

$\mathcal{N}$ovember 25

$\mathscr{M}$y wife invited some people
to dinner. At the table, she turned
to our six-year-old daughter and said,
"Would you like to say the blessing?"
I wouldn't know what to say,"
she replied. "Just say what you hear
Mommy say," my wife said.
Our daughter bowed her head
and said: "Dear Lord,
why on earth did I invite all
these people to dinner?"

November 26

$\mathcal{C}$elebration is more than a happy feeling. Celebration is an experience. It is liking others, accepting others, laughing with others.

DOUGLAS R. STUVA

$\mathcal{N}ovember\ 27$

$\mathcal{H}$umor is one of God's most marvelous gifts. Humor gives us smiles, laughter, and gaiety. Humor reveals the roses and hides the thorns. Humor makes our heavy burdens light and smooths the rough spots in our pathways.

SAM ERVIN

November 28

$\mathcal{I}$'ll never be a millionaire
but I have something better
than that. I have my children,
good friends, a place to call home,
and wonderful relatives. These are
so many of life's wonderful blessings!

$\mathcal{N}ovember\ 29$

*J*ehovah himself is caring for you!
He is your defender. He protects you
day and night. He keeps you from
all evil and preserves your life.
He keeps his eye upon you as you
come and go and always guards you.

PSALM 121:5-8 TLB

November 30

$\mathscr{I}$ have learned that to have
a good friend is the purest of all God's
gifts, for it is a love that has
no exchange of payment.

FRANCES FARMER

$\mathscr{D}ecember\ 1$

$\mathcal{N}$o matter what
the circumstances are,
it is best to pursue behavior
that is above reproach,
because then you will
be respected for your actions.

ROSA PARKS

$\mathcal{D}$ecember 2

$\mathcal{I}$f I can think of myself as loved,
I can love and accept others. If I see
myself as forgiven, I can be gracious
toward others. If I see myself
as powerful, I can do what I know
is right. If I see myself as full,
I can give myself freely to others.

KATHY PEEL

$\mathcal{D}$ecember 3

$\mathscr{L}$ine by line, moment by moment,
special times are etched into our
memories in the permanent ink
of everlasting love in our relationships.

GLORIA GAITHER

December 4

$\mathcal{D}$o you want to stand out?
Then step down. Be a servant.
If you puff yourself up, you'll get
the wind knocked out of you.
But if you're content to simply
be yourself, your life will
count for plenty.

MATTHEW 23:11-12 THE MESSAGE

$\mathcal{D}$ecember 5

*G*od's heart is the most
sensitive and tender of all.
No act goes unnoticed, no matter
how insignificant or small.

RICHARD J. FOSTER

December 6

The beauty of a woman is not
in a facial mole,
But true beauty in a woman
is reflected in her soul.
It is the caring that she lovingly gives,
the passion that she shows,
And the beauty of a woman with
passing years—only grows!

AUDREY HEPBURN

December 7

The supreme characteristic
of courtesy is that thoughtfulness
for others which is the very heart
of Christianity. Schools of etiquette
produce it by training;
love does it by instinct.

HENRY DURBANVILLE

December 8

$\mathscr{L}$aughter dulls the sharpest pain and flattens out the greatest stress. To share it is to give a gift of health because, as someone pointed out, "Ulcers can't grow while you're laughing."

HUNTER "PATCH" ADAMS

December 9

*I*nstead of looking at the fashions,
walk out into the fields and look
at the wildflowers. They never primp
or shop, but have you ever seen color
and design quite like it? The ten best
dressed...women in the country look
shabby alongside them. If God gives
such attention to the appearance
of wildflowers...don't you think he'll
attend to you, take pride in you,
do his best for you?

Matthew 6:28-30 the message

December 10

$\mathcal{W}$hen we are away from God,
He misses us far more
than we miss Him.

RUTH BELL GRAHAM

$\mathcal{D}ecember\ 11$

*T*welve things to remember—
1. The value of time,
2. The success of perseverance,
3. The pleasure of working,
4. The dignity of simplicity,
5. The worth of character,
6. The power of kindness,
7. The influence of example,
8. The obligation of duty,
9. The wisdom of economy,
10. The virtue of patience,
11. The improvement of talent,
12. The joy of origination.

MARSHALL FIELD

December 12

$\mathcal{T}$he answer for satisfying living
for the Christian lies not in organizing,
managing, or controlling life,
but in focusing life.... Life
is simplified when there is one
center, one reason, one motivation,
one direction and purpose.

JEAN FLEMING

$\mathcal{D}$ecember 13

$\mathscr{L}$aughter is like changing a baby's diaper—it doesn't permanently solve any problems, but it makes things more acceptable for a while.

$\mathscr{D}ecember\ 14$

$\mathcal{G}$ive away your life; you'll find life given back, but not merely given back—given back with bonus and blessing. Giving, not getting, is the way. Generosity begets generosity.

LUKE 6:38 THE MESSAGE

$\mathcal{D}$ecember 15

$\mathcal{C}$hristmas, my child, is love in action.... When you love someone, you give to them, as God gives to us. The greatest gift He ever gave was the person of His Son, sent to us in human form so that we might know what God the Father is really like! Every time we love, every time we give, it's Christmas.

DALE EVANS ROGERS

$\mathcal{D}$ecember 16

$\mathcal{A}$t the end of your life you will
never regret not having passed one
more test, not winning one more
verdict, or not closing one more deal.
You will regret time not spent with
a husband, a friend, a child, or a parent.

BARBARA BUSH

December 17

$\mathcal{W}$hen the most important things
in our life happen we quite often
do not know, at the moment,
what is going on.

C. S. LEWIS

$\mathcal{D}$ecember 18

*T*his is what I have asked of God
for you: that you will be encouraged
and knit together by strong ties of
love, and that you will have the rich
experience of knowing Christ
with real certainty and clear
understanding. For God's secret
plan, now at last made known,
is Christ himself.

COLOSSIANS 2:2 TLB

December 19

$\mathcal{Y}$ou who have received so much love show your love by protecting the sacredness of life. The sacredness of life is one of the greatest gifts that God has given us.

MOTHER TERESA

December 20

$\mathcal{G}$od is at home in the play
of His children. He loves
to hear us laugh.

PETER MARSHALL

$\mathcal{D}$ecember 21

$\mathcal{T}$ he fact of Jesus' coming
is the final and unanswerable
proof that God cares.

WILLIAM BARCLAY

December 22

*C*hristmas is the day that
holds all time together.

ALEXANDER SMITH

December 23

The mercy of our God is very tender, and heaven's dawn is about to break upon us, to give light to those who sit in darkness and death's shadow, and to guide us to the path of peace.

LUKE 1:78-79 TLB

December 24

$\mathcal{G}$od grant you the light in Christmas,
which is faith;
the warmth of Christmas,
which is love...
the belief in Christmas,
which is truth;
the all of Christmas,
which is Christ.

WILDA ENGLISH

$\mathcal{D}$ecember 25

$\mathscr{L}$ove is not getting, but giving....
It is goodness and honor and peace
and pure living—yes, love is that
and it is the best thing in the world
and the thing that lives the longest.

HENRY VAN DYKE

December 26

$\mathcal{I}$ believe that nothing that happens
to me is meaningless, and that
it is good for us all that it should
be so, even if it runs counter to our
own wishes. As I see it, I'm here
for some purpose, and I only
hope I may fulfill it. In the light
of the great purpose all our privations
and disappointments are trivial.

DIETRICH BONHOEFFER

$\mathcal{D}$ecember 27

$\mathcal{N}$one of us knows what
the next change is going to be,
what unexpected opportunity is just
around the corner, waiting to change
all the tenor of our lives.

KATHLEEN NORRIS

$\mathcal{D}ecember\ 28$

$\mathcal{Y}$ou have made known to me
the path of life; you will fill me
with joy in your presence, with eternal
pleasures at your right hand.

PSALM 16:11 NIV

December 29

*F*aith isn't the ability to believe long and far into the misty future. It's simply taking God at His word and taking the next step.

JONI EARECKSON TADA

December 30

In the end, I think this is what women truly desire: to know God and to stand tall in their faith, strong at the core, tender in heart.

RUTH SENTER

December 31